MYKLAS CONTEST WINNERS

Original Piano Solos from the Myklas Music Press Library

Foreword

Exciting piano solos are motivating for students, as well as thrilling for audiences. Thoughtfully written and carefully graded original compositions are essential for every piano studio and produce successful learning experiences for students.

Myklas Music Press was highly regarded for its extensive catalogue of quality elementary and intermediate supplemental piano music. The pieces that are included in this volume represent Myklas's most popular and effective solos drawn from festival and contest lists. Divided into four graded collections, outstanding works are made available again by Rhonda Bennett, Ronald Bennett, Rosemary Barrett Byers, Lynne Cox, Anne Shannon Demarest, Mary Hauber, Ernest Kramer, Joyce Schatz Pease, Ruth Perdew, John Robert Poe, Catherine Rollin, Mike Springer, Robert D. Vandall, and Judy East Wells. Their time-tested solos are found on the following pages in approximate order of difficulty.

Contents

Alfred Music Publishing Co., Inc.
P.O. Box 10003
Van Nuys, CA 91410-0003
alfred.com

ISBN-10: 0-7390-7946-8
ISBN-13: 978-0-7390-7946-1

THE MINNOW

Lynne Cox

Playfully

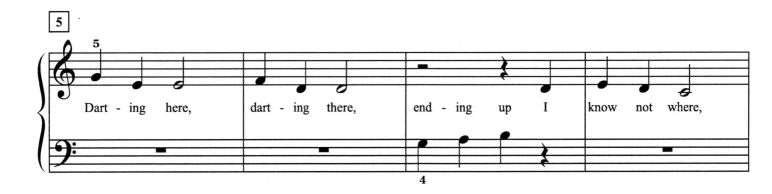

Tee - ny, ti - ny as a snail, you can catch me in a pail.

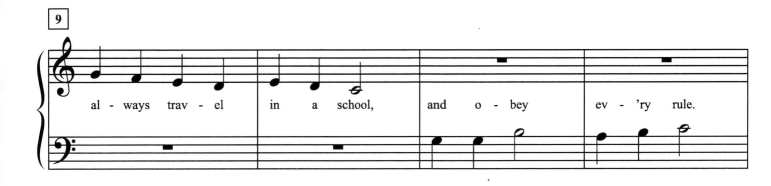

Dart - ing here, dart - ing there, end - ing up I know not where,

al - ways trav - el in a school, and o - bey ev - 'ry rule.

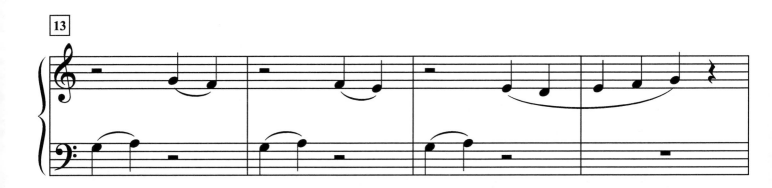

17

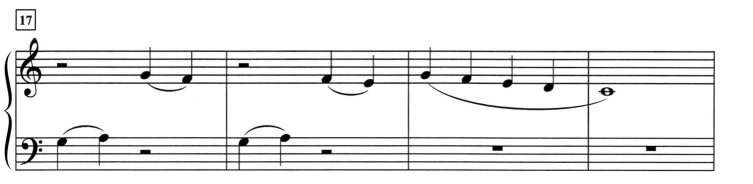

21

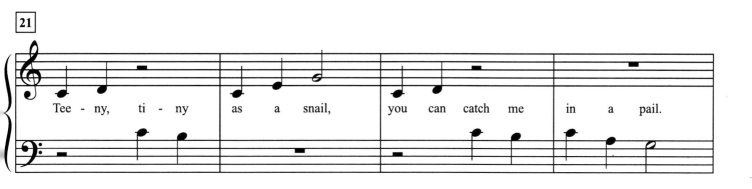

Tee - ny, ti - ny as a snail, you can catch me in a pail.

25

Dart - ing here, dart - ing there, end - ing up I know not where,

29

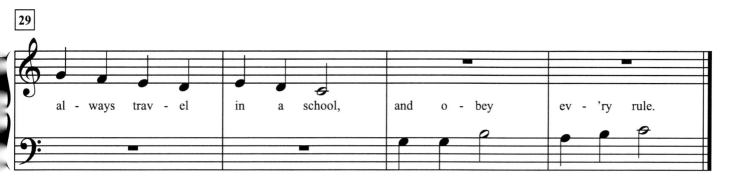

al - ways trav - el in a school, and o - bey ev - 'ry rule.

THE WHALE

Lynne Cox

Boisterously

Oh, what a won - der - ful life I lead,

swim - ming in the sea.

E - ven a might - y pi - rate ship would

stop and look at me. I'm

big and bold (or so I'm told) and

NOW YOU SEE HIM, NOW YOU DON'T!

John Robert Poe

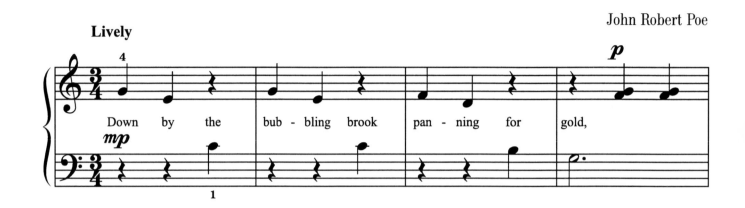

Down by the bub - bling brook pan - ning for gold,

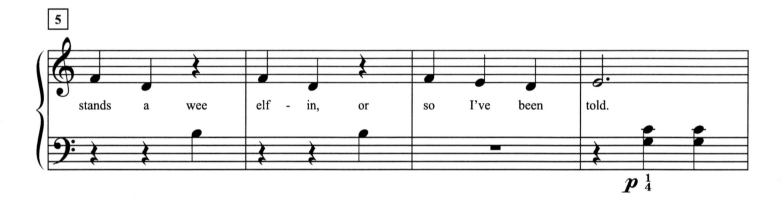

stands a wee elf - in, or so I've been told.

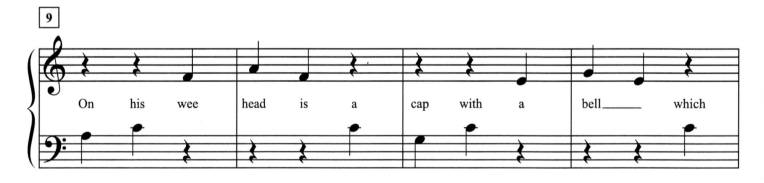

On his wee head is a cap with a bell_____ which

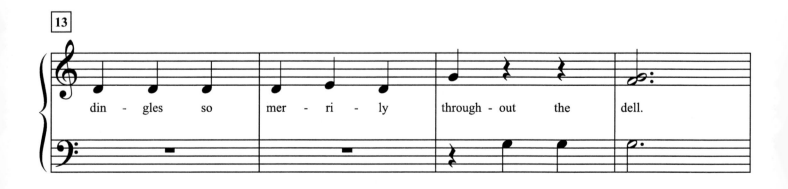

din - gles so mer - ri - ly through - out the dell.

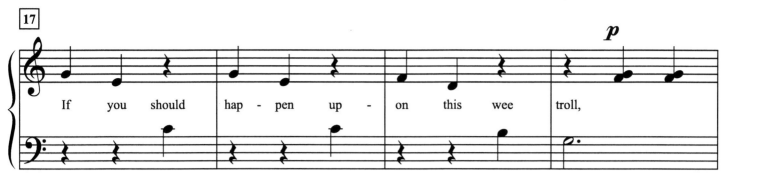

If you should hap - pen up - on this wee troll,

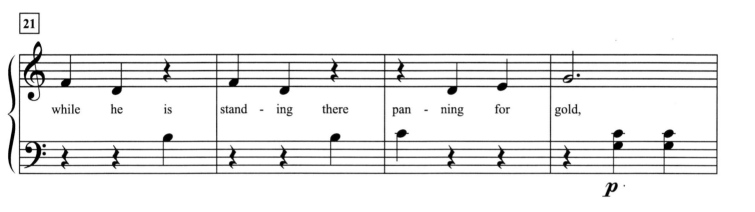

while he is stand - ing there pan - ning for gold,

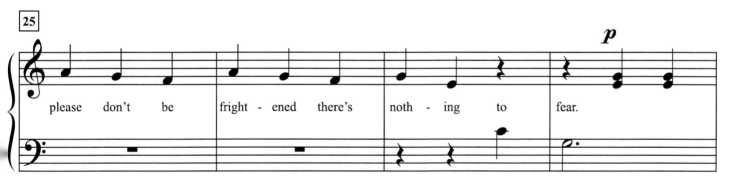

please don't be fright - ened there's noth - ing to fear.

But, if he sees you, he'll soon dis - ap - pear.

CLOWN SERENADE

John Robert Poe

Allegro moderato

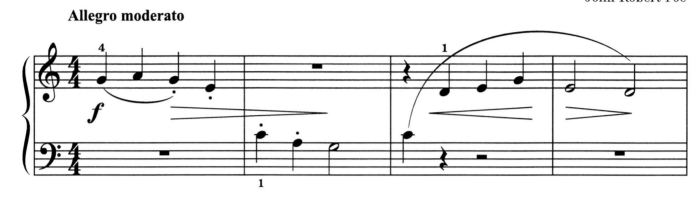

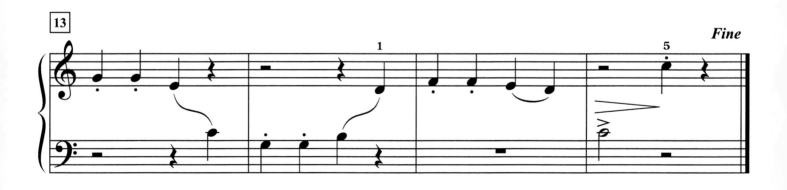

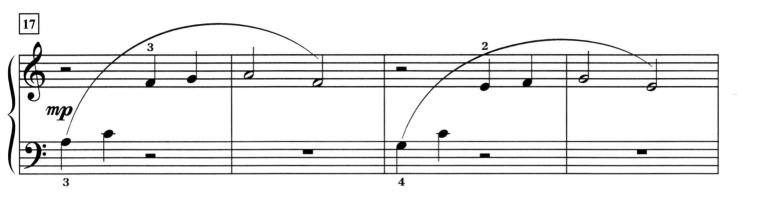

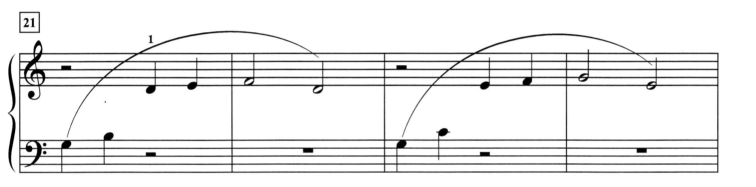

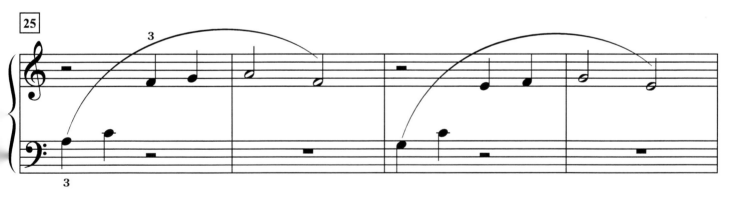

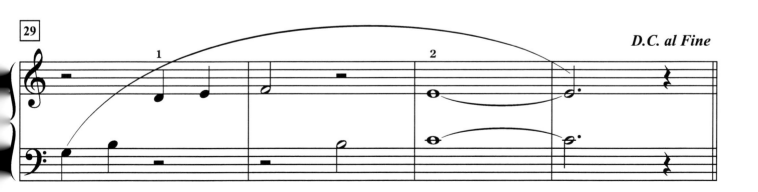

D.C. al Fine

RAIN FOREST

(in Mixolydian mode)

Robert D. Vandall

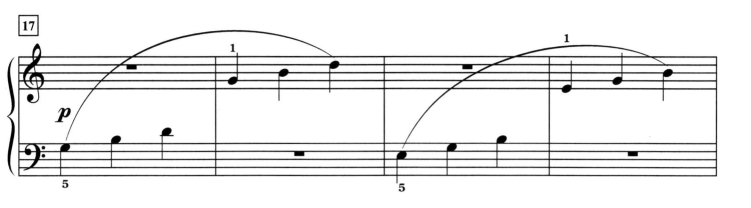

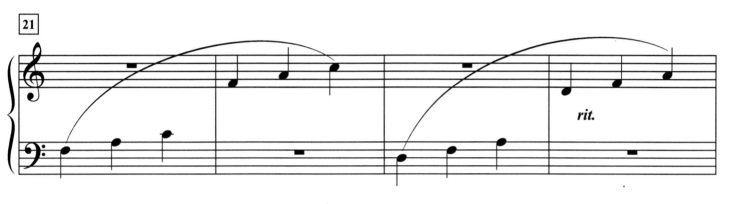

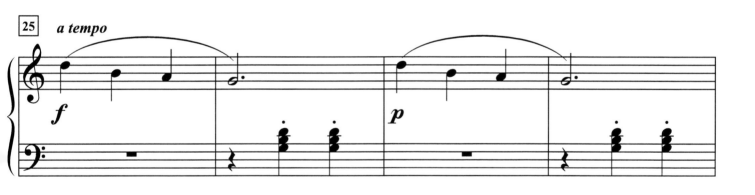

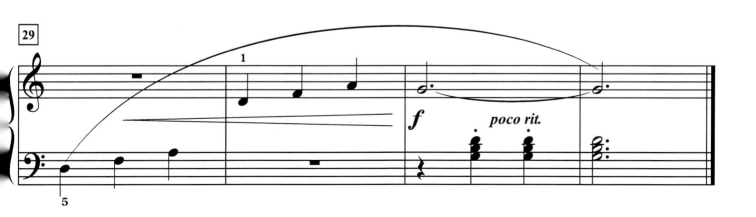

For Sean, Trevor, and Jerry

THE CRAB

Lynne Cox

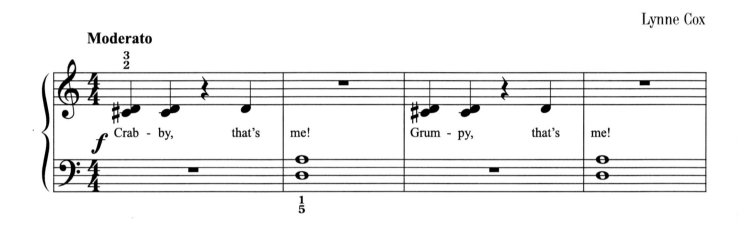

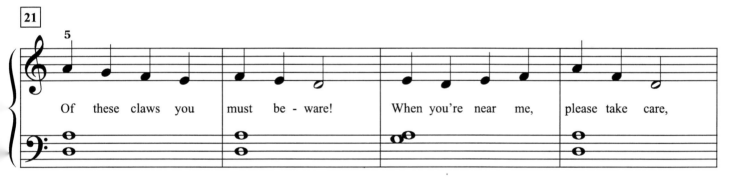

Of these claws you must be - ware! When you're near me, please take care,

or your fin - ger I might snare! SNAP! SNAP! SNAP!

BUBBLE BLUES

Ruth Perdew

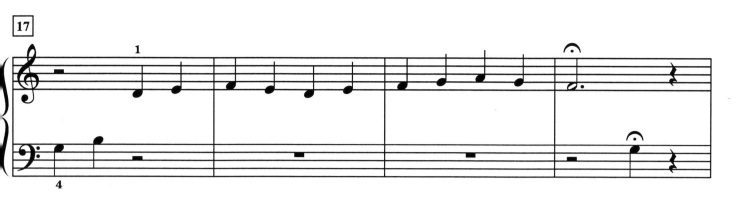

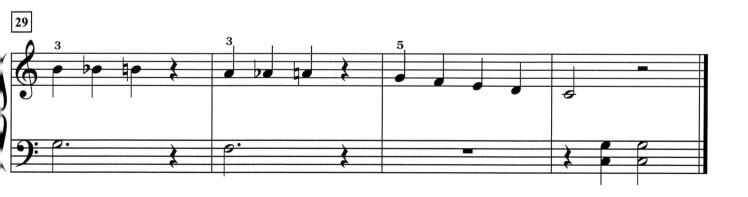

MONKEY BLUES

Ruth Perdew

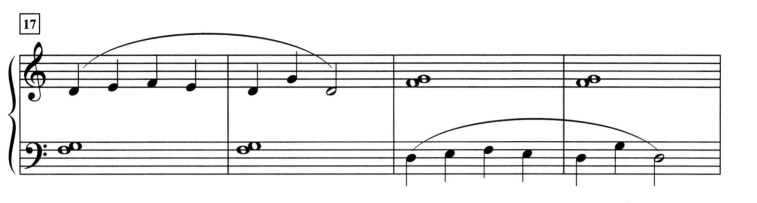

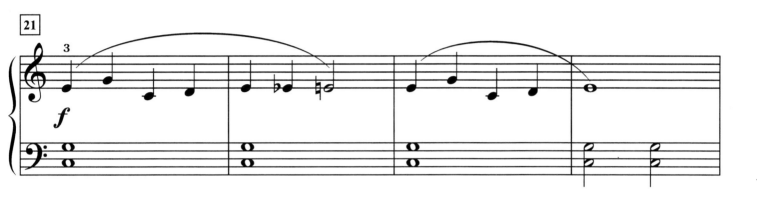

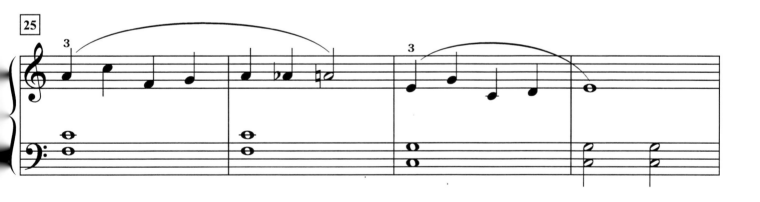

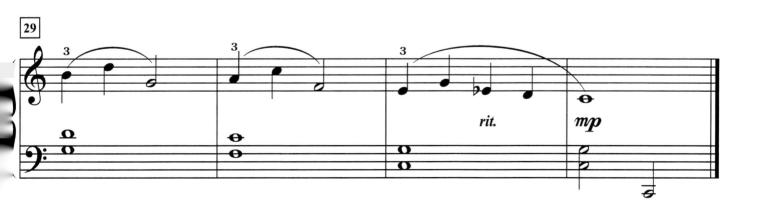

WHO HAS SEEN THE WIND?

Mary Hauber

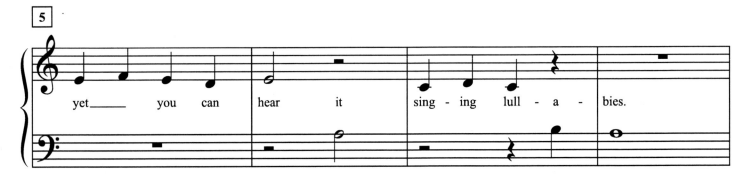

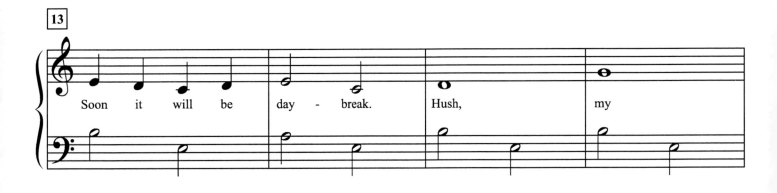

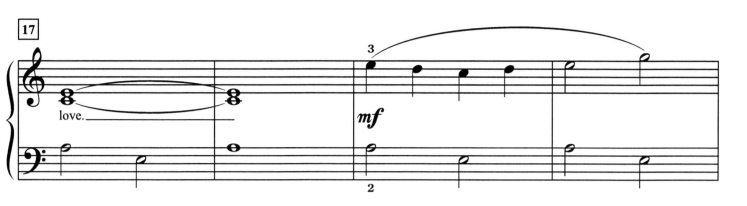

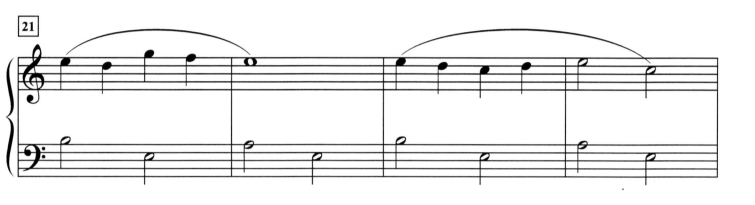

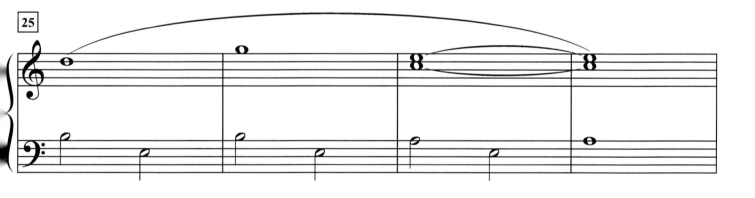

MARCHING TUNE

John Robert Poe

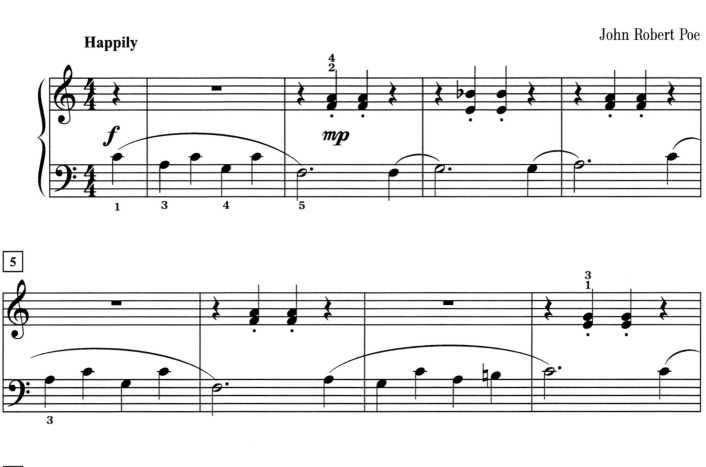

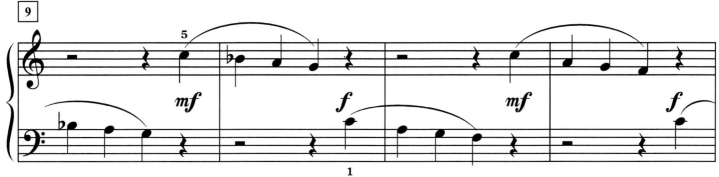

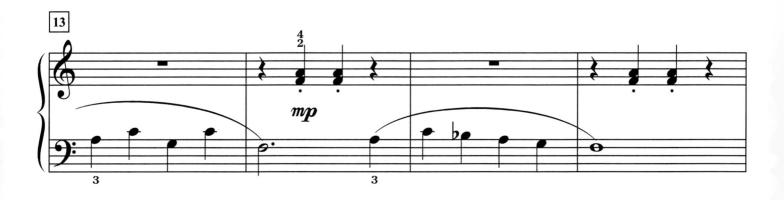

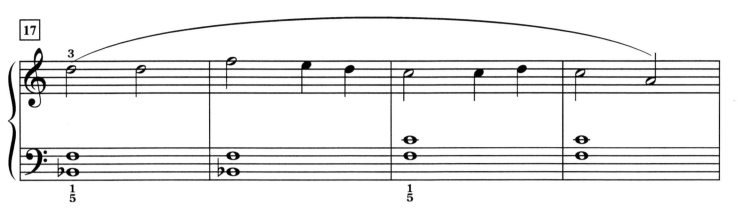

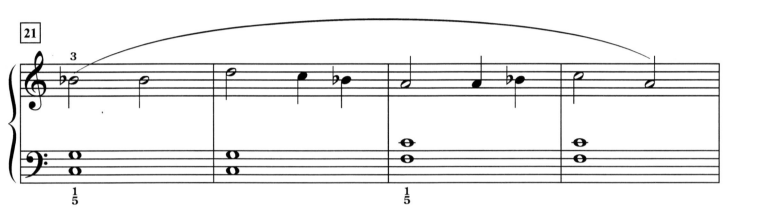

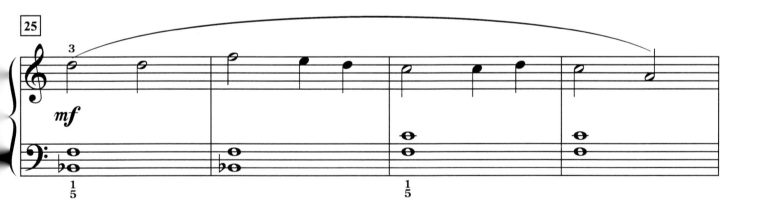

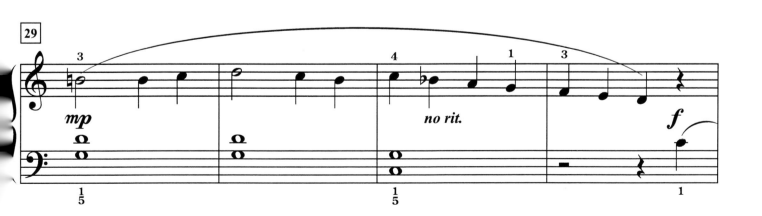

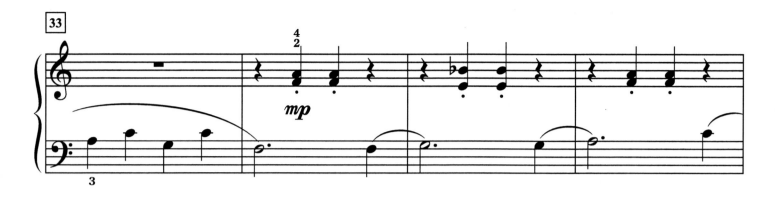

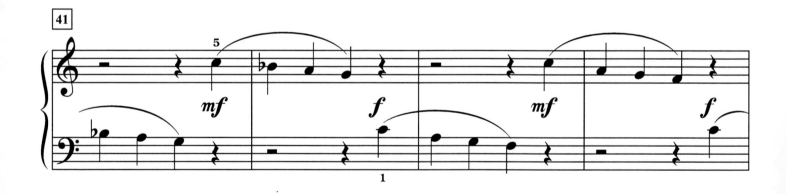

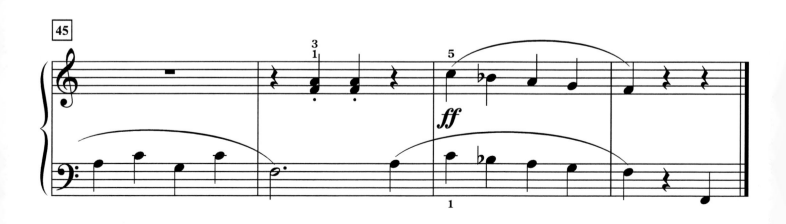

WINDFLOWERS

Anne Shannon Demarest

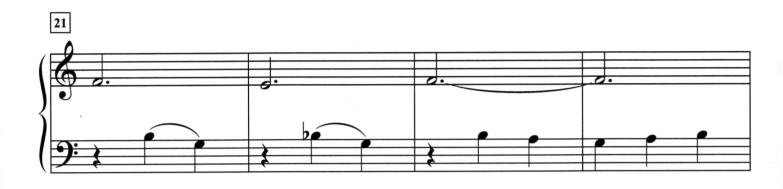

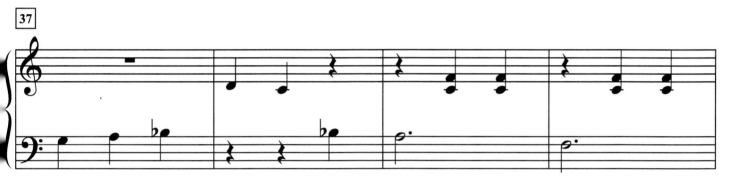

THE LION ROARS

Ruth Perdew

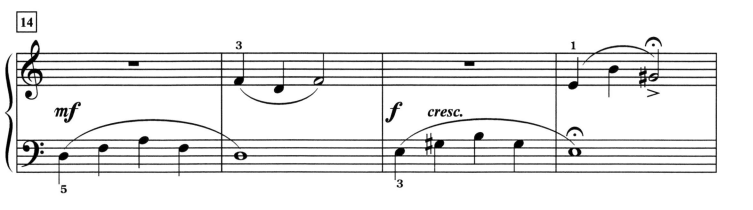

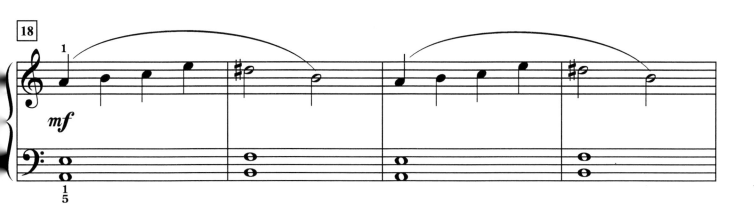

Freely

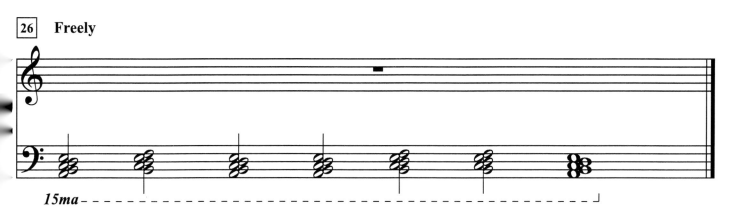

TRUMPET FANFARE

Robert D. Vandall

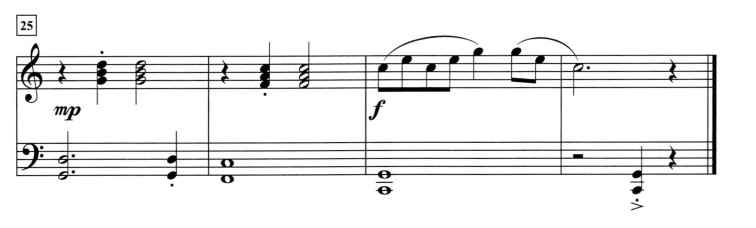

For Christopher Thomas

PANDAS ON PARADE

Ernest Kramer

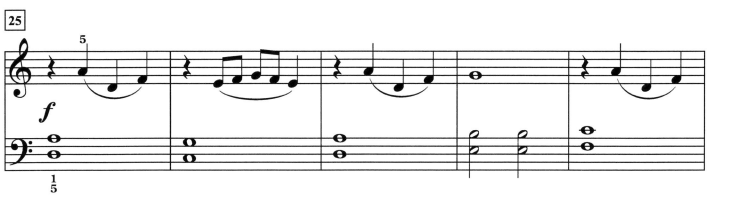

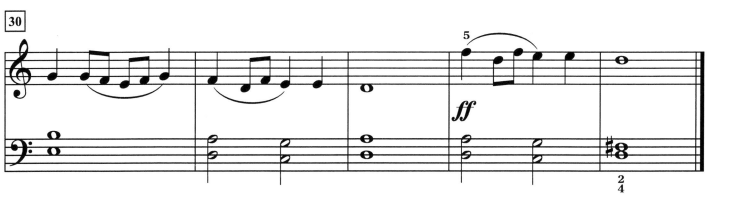